BLAZE

Camouflage and Mimicry:

ANIMAL WEAPONS AND DEFENSES

BY JANET RIEHECKY

CONTENT CONSULTANT:
JACKIE GAI, DVM
ZOO AND EXOTIC ANIMAL VETERINARIAN

READING CONSULTANT:
BARBARA J. FOX
READING SPECIALIST
PROFESSOR EMERITUS
NORTH CAROLINA STATE UNIVERSITY

CAPSTONE PRESS
a capstone imprint

Blazers is published by Capstone Press,
1710 Roe Crest Drive, North Mankato, Minnesota 56003.
www.capstonepub.com

Library of Congress Cataloging-in-Publication Data
Camouflage and mimicry : animal weapons and defenses / by Janet Riehecky.
p. cm. — (Blazers. Animal weapons and defenses)
Includes bibliographical references and index.
Summary: "Describes how animals use camouflage and mimicry as weapons and defenses"—Provided by publisher.
ISBN 978-1-4296-6508-7 (library binding)
ISBN 978-1-4296-8007-3 (paperback)
1. Camouflage (Biology)—Juvenile literature. 2. Mimicry (Biology)—Juvenile literature. I. Title.
QL767.R54 2012
591.47'2—dc23 2011034680

Editorial Credits

Mandy Robbins, editor; Kyle Grenz, designer; Svetlana Zhurkin, media researcher; Laura Manthe, production specialist

Photo Credits

Alamy: Chris Mattison, 10–11, John Cancalosi, 18–19, Robert Shantz, 24–25; Dreamstime: Cigdem Cooper, 12–13, Erectus, 26–27; Getty Images: Joe McDonald, 14–15; iStockphoto: Iggy1108, 8–9; Shutterstock: Audrey Snider-Bell, cover (top), Dennis Donohue, 4–5, RazvanZinica, 6-7, Sari ONeal, cover (bottom), 16–17, Sue Robinson, 22–23; Superstock: Norbert Wu, 20–21; Visuals Unlimited: Joe McDonald, 28–29

Printed in the United States 5904

TABLE OF CONTENTS

NOW YOU SEE IT — NOW YOU DON'T!

Some **predators** and **prey** don't want to be seen. They hide by blending into the background. Other animals want to frighten enemies. They try to look like something big or dangerous.

predator—an animal that hunts other animals for food

prey—an animal that is hunted by another animal for food

HIDING OUT

A bittern uses **camouflage** to hide from predators. The bird stands perfectly still. It looks like a reed sticking up at the water's edge. When the wind blows, the bird sways back and forth.

★ FIERCE FACT ★

The bittern keeps its chest toward enemies. Its back is not camouflaged.

camouflage—coloring or covering that makes animals look like their surroundings

A walking stick is an insect that is hard to spot. When a walking stick stands on a branch, it looks like a stick. When it moves, it **mimics** a twig blown by the wind.

mimic—to copy the looks or behavior of something else

★ FIERCE FACT ★

Young walking sticks can grow a new leg if a predator rips one off.

The horned frog uses camouflage to hide on the jungle floor. The frog looks like a fallen leaf. A predator could walk past without seeing it.

★ FIERCE FACT ★

When hunting, a cuttlefish changes color to distract prey.

A cuttlefish can change color in less than a second. Cuttlefish can even create patterns such as stripes or squares. The patterns help them blend in with their surroundings and hide from predators.

COPYCATS

The scarlet king snake isn't poisonous. But its red, yellow, and black bands mimic those of poisonous coral snakes. Many predators are fooled and keep their distance.

The viceroy butterfly isn't poisonous. But its bright orange colors make it look like the poisonous monarch butterfly. Both butterflies taste bad. Predators learn to avoid orange butterflies.

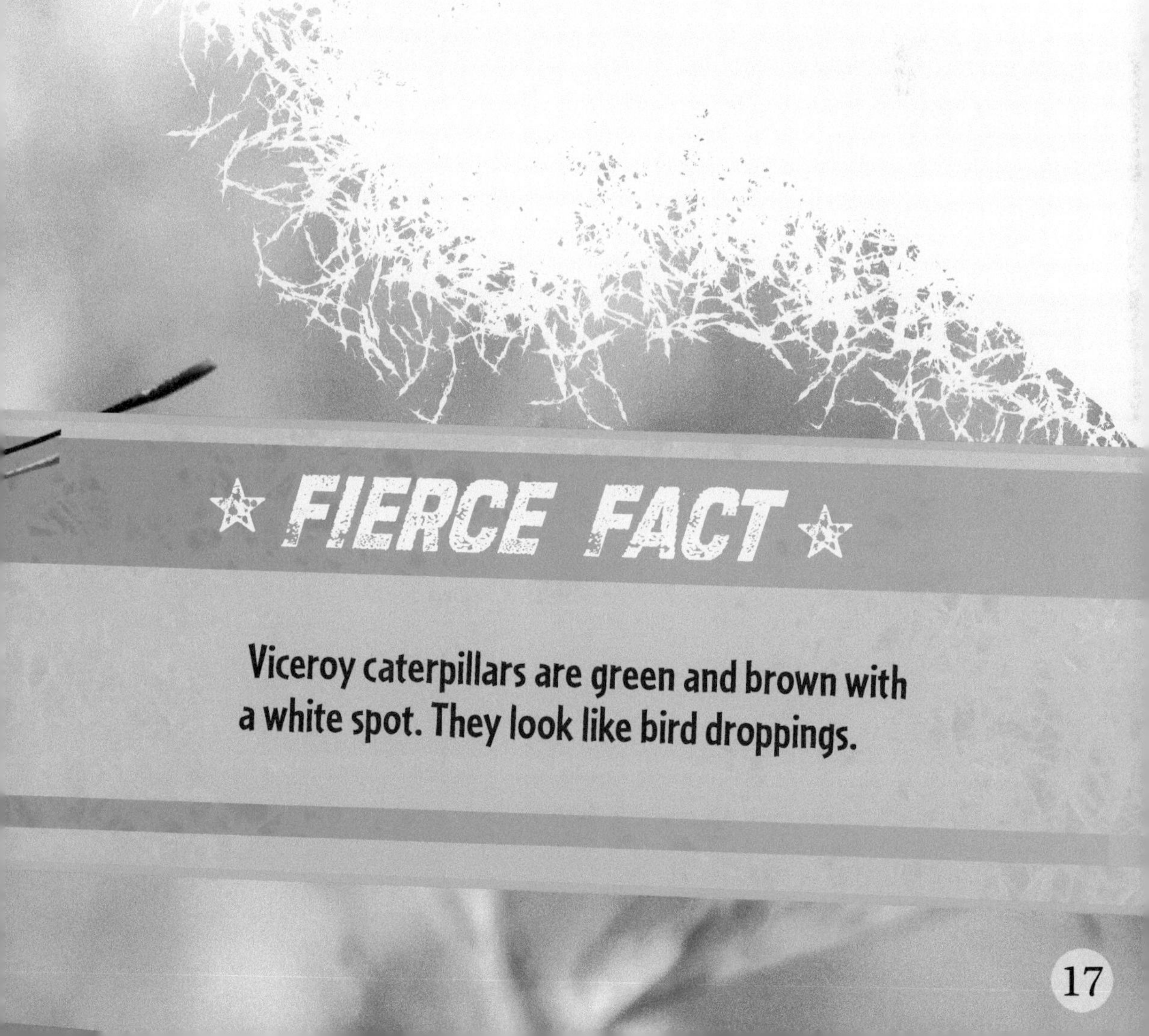

★ FIERCE FACT ★

Viceroy caterpillars are green and brown with a white spot. They look like bird droppings.

Predators are in for a shock when they attack a sphinx moth caterpillar. The caterpillar puffs up its head to look like a snake. Two black spots look like snake eyes.

★ FIERCE FACT ★

The mimic octopus can imitate lionfish, stingrays, and other sea creatures.

The mimic octopus changes its color, shape, and **texture** to look like more dangerous animals. Confused predators leave it alone.

texture—the look and feel of a surface

A SNEAKY AMBUSH

The female flower crab spider doesn't need a web. It changes color to match the flower it's on. Then it sits there, waiting to attack its prey.

★ FIERCE FACT ★

A zone-tailed hawk can see a mouse from a height of 300 feet (91 meters).

Zone-tailed hawks look and act like turkey vultures. But turkey vultures eat wounded or dead animals. Zone-tailed hawks surprise healthy animals and gobble them up.

A polar bear's fur reflects light. This feature makes the bear appear white in the snow. It can blend into the background until prey comes close. Then it pounces!

FIERCE FACT

The alligator snapping turtle can stay underwater for up to 50 minutes.

An alligator snapping turtle has a dark spiky shell. It blends in with mud at the bottom of a lake. The turtle wiggles its tongue to look like a worm. When prey bites, the turtle bites back!

GLOSSARY

ambush (AM-bush)—a sudden, surprise attack

camouflage (KA-muh-flahzh)—coloring or covering that makes animals look like their surroundings

mimic (MIM-ik)—to copy the look, actions, or behaviors of another animal

predator (PRED-uh-tur)—an animal that hunts other animals for food

prey (PRAY)—an animal hunted by another animal for food

reed (REED)—a tall plant with hollow stems that grows in wetlands

texture (TEKS-chur)—the way something feels when you touch it

READ MORE

Helman, Andrea. *Hide and Seek: Nature's Best Vanishing Acts.* New York: Walker & Co., 2008.

Kramer, Jennifer Evans. *Ocean Hide and Seek.* Mount Pleasant, S.C.: Sylvan Dell Pub., 2009.

Mitchell, Susan K. *Animal Mimics: Look-alikes and Copycats.* Amazing Animal Defenses. Berkeley Heights, N.J.: Enslow Pub., 2009.

INTERNET SITES

FactHound offers a safe, fun way to find Internet sites related to this book. All of the sites on FactHound have been researched by our staff.

Here's all you do:

Visit *www.facthound.com*

Type in this code: 9781429665087

www.FactHound.com®

INDEX